Don't Be A Victim

"BE BULLY-FREE!"

~ For the bullied and the fearful ~

By Patrice Lee

Don't Be a Victim, Be Bully-Free

Copyright 2019
Printed in the U.S.A.
1st Revision, May, 2020

This book may not be reprinted, copied, or duplicated in any form including audio, video or other technical format without the express written consent of the publisher.

ISBN #: 978 – 17326210-2-2

Edited by: C. Lee
Cover Design: Bob Ivory, IvoryCoast Media

Feinstein & Associates, d/b/a Leep4Joy Books
P. O. Box 48172, Oak Park, MI 48237

Don't Be a Victim, Be Bully-Free

~ Be Bully-Free ~

Don't Be a Victim, Be Bully-Free

Don't Be a Victim, Be Bully-Free

Book I:

Don't Be a Victim …Be Bully-Free

Table of Contents

Preface 7
Introduction 9
The Bully. 11
The Bully Is a Person 13
Bully History 17
My Friend 23
Tools for Bully-Free Maintenance.. 27
You Don't Have to Fear   31
Seven Principles to Help You   41
A Former Victims' Prayer   48

Don't Be a Victim, Be Bully-Free

Preface

I wrote *"Be Bully-Free"* so you can be free from all the bullies in your life. In this book I share some ancient history to help you recognize some of the similarities in the patterns of behavior of bully character types.

The information is this book is based on the infallible wisdom of the ages, The Holy Bible. It has been said that history often repeats itself. It does.

The Bible is full of history. God's Word says, "There is nothing new under the sun" {Read Ecclesiastes 1:9b}.

Thus, we will examine some of the oldest bullies that ever lived. It may look as though these bullies are winning at first, but if you keep reading, you will see that a bully never wins.

What do we know about bullies? Bullies are unhappy people, and only want to make you miserable so you can be unhappy too. But you need to know that you're only "a victim" if the bully knows you're afraid.

So don't fear. Choose to "live life happy! ! !" Let *"Don't Be a Victim, Be Bully-Free"* help you *"live life on the happy side"* . . .every day.

Don't Be a Victim, Be Bully-Free

Introduction

Did you know you can a peace that surpasses your understanding? If you'd like to have that kind of peace, this book will help you find it.

Even if you've been bullied, or are currently under attack, please know it's only a test. You have something the bully wants, so don't think of yourself as a victim. Let mom, dad, or someone know what you've been experiencing. Please do it today. Share, and keep sharing until the bullying stops.

Now, if you've been wondering, "Who is this bully that keeps bothering me?"

The bully is just a person, or obstacle, that interferes with your happy state of mind. He wants to steal your joy. Therefore, you must find a way to overcome your obstacle.

Choose to see your "bully" as a *virtual* "bully-ball" rolling toward its' target--*you*. And, as in the game of dodge ball, you dodge that ball each time it comes your way.

Avoidance will allow you to have peace of mind until your bully concerns are resolved. Consider yourself a winner, but please let someone know about his{her} actions so the bully can get the help or attention he needs. {See "Special Note from the Author" - pg. 91}.

The Bully . . .

The bully is like a thief who comes in the night. Though he's mean, he doesn't always want ta' fight.

While his purpose is to take away your joy, it serves as mere entertainment for another girl or boy.

Now, if you're looking for the answer, or the next best thing to do, never let this bully know that he's gettin' next to you.

Hold your head up high. Try not to cry. Don't you even fret! Just know it's going to be okay, as you trust God to bring you through the day; and remember to wear a smile, knowing that your bully cares will soon be over in just a little while.

Let God hold you with His righteous right hand, and He'll be your shadow too. And that bully you once feared will gladly find something else to do.

Fear thou not; for I am with thee: be not dismayed; for I am thy God: I will strengthen thee; yea, I will help thee; yea, I will uphold thee with the right hand of my righteousness {Isaiah 41:10}.

"The Bully" is a Person

The bully is just a person like you and me. He has a nose, a mouth and two eyes to see; hands and feet like you and me.

But, the bully's disconnected, feels all alone, 'cause something's not right; . . .could be home.

And when he sees the joy that beams around your face; it makes him feel awkward, kind of out of place.

It magnifies his pain; exposes his hurt. That's why he likes to make you feel like dirt.

Don't Be a Victim, Be Bully-Free

You need not worry or walk in fear. If you tell someone about it, then help is near.

Forgive and release it, so you can *"be happy!"* Forgive and release it so you can be free.

Bullying . . . . .

You need to know and understand bully history, and that this bully activity is nothing new; for bullying didn't start today or yesterday. Oh, the bully's been here for more than a few.

Yes, bullying has been around for a long, long time! So let's go back in ancient history and see what we can find.

For the more you know about it, the stronger you'll be, the sooner you can become completely bully-free.

Don't Be a Victim, Be Bully-Free

Don't Be a Victim, Be Bully-Free

~ Bully History ~

Don't Be a Victim, Be Bully-Free

The Bully Has {a} History

As you read you will see that people were never-always kind; and you'll see that bullies have been with us for a very long, long time. Yes, the bully goes way back.

So turn on your notebook; or get your pen and pad. I'd like to share some of the bully stories I have. It's important that you read each story from beginning to end, for you need to understand that bullies never win.

Most of us know about the first two children recorded in history. They are none other than Cain and Abel. That Cain, the older brother was both a bully and a rebel. You can read about them in Genesis 4:1-8.

~

Next, there's the story of Queen Esther, whose life was in jeopardy by a man from the King's court, named Haman. He was the bully. The Queen's life was threatened, and it looked as though all of her people were going to die; for mean-spirited Haman's plot to kill, also included favorite Uncle, Mordecai. . Her story is in the Book of Esther. See how this Queen risked her life to save her kin. Read about Haman's plot and demise in chapters 3-10. Here, you'll read about his fall, and why he was never heard of again.

Then there was David, the shepherd boy, who became a fearless warrior against both man and beast. As a young boy he had a history of many victories. He knew no defeat. He'd killed a lion, and a bear, all before age ten. Then he gallantly faced Goliath, the giant, the most-feared among men. As a young man David faced the wrath of Saul, a very jealous king; his greatest challenge of all. See how David had to run for his life for many years because Saul, the King, wanted him dead. This fascinating story begins in 1 Samuel 19. You'll see that God had better plans for him instead.

~

The story is a little different when it comes to Apostle Paul. For when he began his journey, his name was also Saul. Known as Saul of Tarsus, he persecuted others and brought great harm to all. Then suddenly one day, when he was knocked off his horse, he lost his sight and went tumbling to the ground. His story is found in Acts 8: 1-3, Acts 9:1-27, and Acts 13:9. Read and see how his life was completely turned around. Paul opened doors for you and me. Paul became a great man in God's kingdom. He made history.

~

My Friend. . .

There are many more stories of bullies, but, the next one is special to me. It's about a dear friend who was bullied terribly.

He was very kind, and full of love. He had many friends, but, no one could protect Him from His bullies 'til His journey's end. In fact, they didn't even try.

Oh, how they beat and shoved Him, mocked, and called Him out of name. They shouted and cursed Him, and ripped His clothes to shame. But, this was a part of His journey from heaven to earth, to fulfill His purpose, redeem us, and give us worth.

Don't Be a Victim, Be Bully-Free

With a crown of thorns on His head, and nails pierced in His side, He hung there, on Calvary's cross, . . .said, "It is finished!" Then He died.

He did it for you and for me, to give us eternal life, to set us free; so we could live with Him throughout eternity.

Will you accept His friendship invitation today? Let Him have first place in your life. Don't delay!

~

"The thief cometh not, but for **to steal**, and **to kill**, and **to** destroy: I am come that they might have life, and that they might have it more abundantly"(John 10:10b).

~

...Wants To Be Your Friend Too

God wants to give you peace beyond your understanding, and fill your heart with unspeakable joy. If you'd like to accept His invitation for a personal relationship with Jesus, by receiving Him as your Lord and Savior, please say this prayer out loud:

"Dear Heavenly Father, I am a sinner. I believe that you gave your only Son, Jesus, that I might be saved. I repent of my sin, and turn away from it now. Lord Jesus, come into my heart and save me now? Right now I am born again, in Jesus' Name. Amen."

Understanding Salvation

"For all have sinned, and come short of the glory of God; being justified freely by His grace through the redemption that is in Christ Jesus" {Romans 3:23-24}.

"For God so loved the world, that He gave His only begotten Son, that whosoever believeth in Him should not perish, but have everlasting life" {John 3:16}.

"If we confess our sins, He is faithful and just to forgive us our sins, and to cleanse us from all unrighteousness" {1 John 1:9}.

"...if thou shalt confess with thy mouth the Lord Jesus, and shalt believe in thine heart that God hath raised Him from the dead, thou shalt be saved. For with the heart man believeth unto righteousness; and with the mouth confession is made unto salvation" {Romans 10:9-10}.

Tools for Bully-Free Maintenance

Don't Be a Victim, Be Bully-Free

Now that you've received Jesus as your Lord, know that He has good things in store for you, and wants you to have good success. All of the tools you need to succeed can be found in His Word –The Holy Bible.

"Tools" from the "Toolkit"

Mechanics or repairmen are often recognized by their tools. "Tools" are used to help fix what is broken, repair things, or patch them up. "Tools" help you maintain what you have, put things in order, and make them right again.

Some "tools" are known for their power; some are known for their strength, and some "tools" are very sharp. The Bible is our "tool" book, and is all of the above.

It is *strengthening, powerful,* and *sharp.* It is one of the greatest "tools" a Christian can have to keep life in order.

God's Word becomes even more powerful when we read, study, meditate, and say the verses out loud. For it activates the spirit within us to respond to what it hears us speak.

His Word - our "tool" book restores life, and brings health and wholeness to our mind and body again. It helps us think on good reports and good things, both lovely and just.

The Holy Bible can be used as a guide to encourage us and help us succeed in every area of life. His promises can bring the positive change we desire. Apply the "tools" {His Word} today, and trust Him in everything.

Don't Be a Victim, Be Bully-Free

You Don't Have to Fear

Don't Be a Victim, Be Bully-Free

Fear Not. . .

<u>Fear</u>: What does God have to say about it? The phrase "Fear not" can be found many times in The Bible. Here's what God's Word says: *"For God has not given us the spirit of fear, but of power, and of love and of a sound mind"* {2 Timothy 1:7}.

He not only tells us not to fear, if we have been wronged, mistreated, or bullied, but promises to do something on our behalf. The Bible also says, *"Fret not thyself because of evildoers, neither be thou envious against the workers of iniquity. For they shall soon be cut down like the grass, and wither as the green herb"* {Psalm 37:1-2}. God also says, *"...Vengeance is mine; I will repay..."* {Romans 12:19b}.

There is nothing more powerful than the words I read on one of the most challenging days of my life. On this day, I opened my Bible to a page of scripture verses I'd never seen before that read:

"Fear thou not; for I am with thee {you}: be not dismayed; for I am thy {your}God: I will strengthen thee {you}; yea, I will help thee {you}; yea, I will uphold thee {you} with the right hand of my righteousness" {Isaiah 41: 10}

And there was more as I kept reading, *"For I the Lord thy God will hold thy right hand, saying unto thee, Fear not; I will help thee* {Isaiah 41: 13}. And more…, *"Fear not, …I will help thee saith the Lord…"* {Isaiah 41:14}.

These promises changed my life, increased my faith, and gave me hope. Promise me you'll look up these important verses of scripture and read them (out loud). Something happens when you read The Word of God aloud. It comes alive, takes root on the inside of you; and the more you say it, the stronger you become.

My friend, God is love. He is perfect love. And perfect love cast out all fear. In Him and through Christ Jesus, you can reject fear, and replace it with love. Speak to your fear. Command it to go now, in Jesus name.

Don't Be a Victim, Be Bully-Free

~ Getting Dressed for Battle ~

Sometimes life is smooth, peaceful, easygoing, serene… And sometimes it's like an obstacle course, where the terrain is rough, rugged, or uneven. The bully was my obstacle in the workplace. When I arrived each day, he showed up.

There were many bullies there, so I needed special protection. Regardless of size or number, I had to be fully clothed in righteousness to withstand the pressure.

What we wear says a lot about us, both spiritually and physically. Even the colors we choose–whether bright and bold, or soft and subdued, our clothing will let people know something about us.

As a Christian, it was my responsibility to be clothed in my righteous armor daily, for it gave God authority in the earth realm to fight on my behalf. Since this was a spiritual battle, I had to follow God's instruction and put my spiritual garments on for Him to protect me from all evil. {Read Ephesians 6:10 – 18.} Say it every day.

When I had my armor on, no one could still my joy. And when I let God battle the bullies, I was always victorious. We always win with Jesus.

So put your armor on!

~ Speak the Word –Only ~

Why is it important to speak the Word? The scriptures you read, and the words you speak are very powerful. God responds to His Word, when we speak it. So, we must be careful to speak only His Word if we want to continue to have a victorious outcome.

Reminding God of His Word causes Him to move on our behalf, for He wants us to have every promise for which He has made provision. So speak the Word, and believe what you say as you speak it!

Don't Be a Victim, Be Bully-Free

Seven Principles to Help You Live Life Victoriously

Don't Be a Victim, Be Bully-Free

Seven Steps to Victory

1. Forgive those who have come against you; and forgive instantly.

2. Find the scripture or Bible promise that matches what you're believing God for.

3. Say (read) His promise(s) out loud.

4. Refuse to doubt. Believe what God's Word says. "Believe only" {Luke 8:50}.

5. Have faith. Because you believe, you can thank God in advance. This will activate your faith.

6. Expect to have, and enjoy peace; for peace follows this kind of faith.

7. As others notice the changes in your life, they'll wonder what you are doing. ☺

Scripture references for each step:

1. "Forgive, and ye shall be forgiven" {Luke 6:37b}.
2. "So shall my word be that goeth forth out of my mouth: it shall not return unto me void…" {Isaiah 55:11a}.
3. "..not doubt, but shall believe.., he shall have whatsoever he saith" {Mark 11:23}.
4. "Believe only" {Luke 8:50}.
5. "Now faith is the substance of things hoped for, the evidence of things not seen" {Hebrews 11:1}.
6. "He will keep you in perfect peace, as you keep your mind stayed on Him" {reference: Isaiah 26:3}.
7. "…Behold, all things are become new" {2 Corinthians 5:17}.

Don't Be a Victim, Be Bully-Free

A Special Kind of Love –

Jesus, has a special kind of love for all mankind. It's called "unconditional love." It helps us love without limits or conditions. When we learn to love His way, we really don't mind doing it.

Your daily decision to forgive someone who isn't kind helps expand your capacity to love unconditionally. As you practice immediate forgiveness and add to it love, you too, will be bully-free.

It's love without limitations, where you love no matter what. It's being kind to those who've done you wrong, and letting by-gones. . .be gone.

As you choose to love others in this special kind of way, you add peace, favor, and countless blessings to your life each day.

Everyone needs to be loved, bullies need it too. Enduring the pain and disappointment as we love without limits; that's what it takes to get us through.

~ Noah Webster defines "unconditional" as absolute, unreserved.' I prefer to describe it as "without conditions or limitations." Then, "unconditional love" is loving with-out reservation or limitation. It is absolute love.

"To the bully who bullied me, I want to share some good news:

'Today, **I** choose to **love you** - unconditionally!
And **I choose** to **forgive** you too.'

Now my thoughts are clear, for
I know it's not my fault that you lunged at me.

For it's through forgiveness that I can love you, find healing, and be a better me.

It doesn't matter that you bullied me -
You are forgiven!
I have released you!
Now I'm free to laugh again,
And just be me."

A Former Victim's Prayer:

"Dear Lord, I humble myself before You. I put my trust in You. I forgive the bully, for all the things he's put me through. No matter what he's done; I choose to walk in love. I choose to follow You." :)

The capacity to love is far greater than the one for fear, when you trust God with all your heart and keep Him near. Stay in His presence.

"...Let us love one another..." (1 John 4: 7b)

Don't Be a Victim, Be Bully-Free

May these *scripture* references keep you strong in your *love-walk:*

"Fret not thyself because of evildoers, neither be thou envious against the workers of iniquity. For they will soon be cut down like the grass, and wither as the green herb" {Psalm 37:1 -2}.

"For God has not given us {me} the spirit of fear, but of power, and of love, and of a sound mind" {2 Timothy 1:7}.

"The Lord is my light and my salvation; whom shall I fear? The Lord is the strength of my life; of whom shall I be afraid?" {Psalm 27:1}

"God is our {my} refuge and strength, a very present help in trouble" {Psalm 46:1}.

"God is the strength of my heart..." {Psalm 73:26b}.

"For thou hast girded me with strength unto the battle, thou hast subdued under

Don't Be a Victim, Be Bully-Free

me those who rose up against me" {Psalm 18:39}.

"Cast all your care upon Him, for He cares. . ." {You can say, "I cast all of my care upon You Father God."} {1 Peter 5:7}.

"...forgive, and ye shall be forgiven" {Luke 6:37b}.

"I will trust in the Lord with all of my heart. . ." {refer to Proverbs 3:5a}.

"In thee, O Lord, do I put my trust" {Psalm 31:1a}

"Thou shalt love thy neighbor as thyself" {Mark 12:31b}.

"I can do all things through Christ which strengthens me" {Philippians 4:13}.

"...be strong in the Lord, and in the power of His might" {Ephesians 6:10b}

Don't Be a Victim, Be Bully-Free

Don't Be a Victim, Be Bully-Free

Don't Be a Victim, Be Bully-Free

Unconditional **"Bully Love"**

~ for bullies too ~

By **Patrice Lee**

'

Don't Be a Victim, Be Bully-Free

Don't Be a Victim, Be Bully-Free

Book II:

Unconditional "Bully-Love"

Table of Contents

Introduction 57

Unconditional "Bully-Love". 61

A Bully's Prayer 67

Increase Your Capacity to Love. . 69

Activating "Love" 73

Just One More Thing 79

Epilogue 87

Don't Be a Victim, Be Bully-Free

Don't Be a Victim, Be Bully-Free

Introduction

Bullies have a lack of something in their lives. For many of them, it's love. Therefore, we must always respond in love. A kind response for the bully can be life changing, because even the meanest person responds to "love."

When you practice "unconditional love," you can extend kindness to everyone, including the bully. I call it "unconditional bully-love."

There is no fear in "love."

~ "Unconditional love" - loving others with-out reservation or limitation. It is absolute love.

Don't Be a Victim, Be Bully-Free

~ Good News for the Bully ~

Dear Bully,

"I want to share some good news:

I forgive you.
Today, **I'm choosing** to **love you** - unconditionally!

It doesn't matter anymore that you bullied me - 'Cause **you** are **forgiven,**

I've released you.
Now, I am free.

And I am happy with who I am . . .just being me!"

.

Unconditional **"Bully-Love"**

When I showed the bully love-unconditional, he simply went away. And suddenly, it was a much better day.

The bully became silent as if to disappear. For he walked away speechless; and with his silence went my fear.

Then, more love entered in, pouring from above. 'Til my body, mind, and soul was drenched in fearless love.

Love is greater than fear. Empowered from above, even the meanest person responds to the purest form of love.

Choose "love!"

Don't Be a Victim, Be Bully-Free

A Touch of Unconditional
"Bully-Love"

Don't Be a Victim, Be Bully-Free

"Love Message" to the Bully

To anyone, boy or girl, who is, or has been a bully: There's "good news" for you.

God has placed good inside of you. He wants you to discover those gifts and use them, so He can be proud of you. He wants you to be happy too.

But, you'll have to release all pride, to let go of all the pain you've held inside, so you can be clean within, and feel good again.

Maybe someone has said something mean, or bullied you; made you feel unloved, or accused you falsely for something you didn't do.

Maybe you've felt rejected, or felt least adored. Perhaps, in your life you've been ignored. Forgive and release it. Receive help from above. Let God fill your heart with His unconditional love.

Let this be the day for reconciliation; to release all pain, or change affiliations. Open your heart to release your troubled past. Let ill-feelings part.

Forgiveness is something you must do, 'cause Bully, you need forgiveness too. As you forgive others, forgiveness comes right back to you.

Then, choose to live life bully-free. Choose to forgive and love – unconditionally!

∼

"...forgive, and ye shall be forgiven" {Luke 6:37b}.

"...for whatsoever a man soweth, that shall he also reap" {Galatians 6:7}.

Don't Be a Victim, Be Bully-Free

A "**Bully's Prayer**"

To every man, woman, boy or girl, who is, or was a bully, you need to know that you can have peace and be filled with a love that's real, one that last forever.

But, first, you must ask to be forgiven. You can say it in a prayer {like this}.

Dear Heavenly Father,

Today I ask you to forgive me for hurting others and crushing dreams. Forgive me for the words I spoke, the physical things I did, the little jokes.

Forgive me for anything I may have said

or done that brought harm to others, if only one.

Jesus, you gave your life that I might live. Now my heart to You I give. As I submit my will to You, cleanse me, purge me; make all things new.

Thank you for saving me, so I can love –unconditionally too. I pray in Jesus' Name. Amen.

~

Now my friend, remember, that you are loved with an unerring love – unconditionally.

Increase Your Capacity to **Love**

Love yourself.

Why is it so important to love yourself? . . .so you can love others. Because it's impossible to love someone else, or even try, if you don't have self-love.

The Bible says, "Love your neighbor as you love yourself" (Read Mark 12:30-31). As you learn to love the way God loves, you will become a better person and neighbor too.

That means you must treat yourself kindly, think good thoughts about you, and even say nice things about yourself as well. Eventually, you'll make a believer out of yourself as you continue to think and say these good things.

Seeds of **Faith** Help Faith *Grow*

Here's something you need to know. When fear is present, "faith seeds" can't "grow." Use God's Word to conquer fear. Read it and believe each word you hear.

To "grow" in "faith," you'll need to read The Holy Bible through and through. Just keep your eyes on the Book, 'til it sticks like glue.

The "seeds of faith" you plant in His Word, will cause your "faith" to "grow." Stand on His promises and say what God says until you see – *It's so! ! !*

As you "grow" in "faith," you'll have a new attitude. Let the Psalms and Proverbs be your {new} comfort food. The closer you get to Him, the stronger you'll be, developing a capacity to "forgive and love" everyone.

Don't Be a Victim, Be Bully-Free

Activating **"Love"**

Don't Be a Victim, Be Bully-Free

New Day, New Start

Don't Be a Victim, Be Bully-Free

I'll begin each day with prayer and meditate on God's Word. His Word gives me peace and strength.

Today I will increase my capacity to love, by (See the list below.):

1. _____ _____

   _____

2. _____

   _____

3. _____

   _____

4. _____

   _____

5. _____

   _____

6. _____

   _____

7. _____

Be an example of love in action. Here are some ways to show love:

- Be kind to myself
- Be kind in conversations
- Support others in need
- Give someone a helping hand
- Make someone smile. Share yours.
- Smile, even when you don't feel like it, for one smile can change the atmosphere.

Don't Be a Victim, Be Bully-Free

These are the ways I can show "love…"

1. _____

   _____

2. _____

   _____

3. _____

   _____

4. _____

   _____

5. _____

   _____

Don't Be a Victim, Be Bully-Free

6. _____

   _____

7. _____

   _____

8. _____

   _____

9. _____

   _____

10. _____

    _____

Just One More Thing...

Don't Be a Victim, Be Bully-Free

Something Else You Need to Know…

God *…forgives when you ask Him to.* When you repent {of all sin} and ask God for forgiveness, you are truly "forgiven." Yes. He forgives you, just like that. *"…Thy sins are forgiven"* {Luke 7:48b}.

…Keeps no record. When God forgives, He doesn't hold a grudge. Instead, He wipes the slate clean, and keeps no record of any wrong you've done. That's right. He cleanses you from sin and washes the thought of it away too. Isn't He awesome? *"There is no remembrance of former things; neither shall there be any remembrance of things that are to come with those that shall come after"* {Ecclesiastes 1:11}.

...Is your Security. "*...The Lord is my rock, and my fortress, and my deliverer;*" {2 Samuel 22:2b}. Is your security in material possessions or people? Objects and people can disappear in an instant. But, Jesus Christ is "*...the same yesterday, and today, and forever*" {Hebrews 13:8}. He said, "*For I am the Lord, I change not;*" {Malachi 3:6}.

...Thinks you're special. God always has your best interest at heart. He is your protector {safety net}. He says, "*I will uphold you with my righteous right hand...*" {Reference Isaiah 41:10b}. So just "*Cast... all of your care upon Him; for He careth for you*" {Reference: 1 Peter 5:7}.

...Gives peace. God wants to fill your days with endless peace. This means that no matter what's going on in your life, around you, or in the world, you can still have peace. And *"He will keep you in perfect peace, if you keep your mind stayed on Him..."* {Reference: Isaiah 26:3}.

Trust Him. God promises that He *"...will never leave you nor forsake you"* {Hebrews 13:5b}. You can enjoy a victorious life if you put your faith and trust in Jesus. You can completely lean on, and rely on Him. *"Trust in the Lord with all of thine heart; and lean not unto thine own understanding"* {Proverbs 3:5}. *"I will be with you alway{s}, even until the end of the earth..."* {Reference: Matthew 28:20}.

His desire… God wants you to spend time with Him. He wants your praise, a one-on-one conversation, and your love. He wants to be glorified in everything you do. *"Delight thyself. . . in the Lord; and He shall give thee the desires of thine heart."* {Psalm 37:4a}.

It's a Brand New Day. Every day in Christ Jesus is brand new; fresh. And if you mess up today, ask Him to forgive you. Then, forgive yourself, and know that tomorrow is a brand new day. *"Therefore, if any man be in Christ, he is a new creature: old things are passed away; behold, all things are become new"* {2 Corinthians 5:17}.

Be Free! Refresh your mind daily with good thoughts, and think on whatever is true, honest, pure, lovely, or just.

Always look for a good report. You'll feel better, lighthearted and free. {Read Philippians 4:8}

Laugh. For God has a sense of humor. He wants to see you smile, laugh and have fun. *"A merry heart doeth good like a medicine. . ."* {Proverbs 17:22}.

Peace! Peace! Wonderful Peace! *"...the peace of God, which passeth all understanding, shall keep your hearts and minds through Christ Jesus"* *{*Philippians 4:7*}.* Choose to wake up each morning in God's presence, and you'll be surrounded by peace--a peace that surpasses all understanding.

Go in peace! And be free! ! !

~

Don't Be a Victim, Be Bully-Free

"Those things you have both learned, and received, …do, and the God of peace shall be with you" {Philipp. 4:9}.

Epilogue:

I hope the message in Book I: *"Don't Be a Victim, Be Bully-Free"* and Book II: *"Unconditional Bully-Love"* have been life-changing for you. I encourage you to continue to read The Holy Bible and allow it to bring transformation in your life.

My friend, continue to speak the Word of God over your life and remember to "<u>*Say something*</u>*!*" Talk to God about all of your concerns; and know that He cares about everything. Freedom is life-changing.

God promises blessing for those who choose to obey His Word; consequences for those who do not. If we have love in our heart, we express that love through our words, deeds, and actions.

It's better to obey God's instruction, and walk in a loving way with our neighbor, to forgive-instantly, and live peaceably with our fellow man, than to harbor bitterness, jealousy, anger, or hatred in our heart for others.

To the children/youth: When you encounter a "bully" or mean-spirited person, tell someone you trust. Speak up the first time something happens{to you}, or each time you feel threatened. Then, the "bully" can get the attention he needs and make the world a better place in which to live.

Now for those who still need to be convinced that bullying isn't acceptable, please take time to read the following passages from the Word of God:

{_Blessings of obedience_:}
Deuteronomy 8:1-14

{_Consequences of disobedience_:}
Deuteronomy 8:15-68; Obadiah 1:3-4; Obadiah 1:10; Proverbs 6:16-19; Psalm 37: 1-40

~

Special Note from the Author

Oh how I loved the game of dodge ball when we got to play it in gym class. For some reason I felt so invigorated each time I dodged that ball coming toward me.

When I experienced bullying in the workplace, I began to look for a way of escape. Somehow the game of mental dodge ball became that escape mechanism for me.

During this difficult period in my life I envisioned my bully as a kind of ball rolling toward me. Every time I saw this "bully-ball" coming my way, I avoided it. Each time I avoided contact with him, I felt like a winner. ☺ So, the next time you see a "bully-ball" coming your way, dodge the ball.

About the Author:

Patrice Lee is an author, publisher, speaker, freelance writer. She loves people, has a great appreciation for music and the arts, and is a survivor of "workplace bullying."

Her books are designed to help children, teens, and adults have inner peace, spiritual growth, and personal success. "Writing is my opportunity to pay it forward, by helping others rise above their negative 'circumstance, and accept each day as a gift." She encourages others to 'Live life on the happy side.' ~ Read a Leep4Joy book.

Don't Be a Victim, Be Bully-Free

~

If you like this **Leep4Joy** book, we have more. . . ☺ Please see the list below:

Happy To Be Me!
The Bully Met My Dad! …Became My Friend
Let's Love One Another
It's Just A CIRCUMSTANCE!
I Like Who I Am I Love Being Me
It's About the "BOYS!"

Bully Me? …No More!!!{Bully me? ...no mas!}
Bully Me? …Oh No!!!
How to Overcome Every Obstacle ...Land on Top {also en Espanol}

Mommy, …Are You Listening? ? ?
Daddy! …Can YOU Hear Me? ? ?
Tips & Tools for a Safe and Healthy School Yr

Stay tuned for more "Good News," for more "Good News" is coming soon. ☺

~

www.ingramcontent.com\pod-product-compliance
Lightning Source LLC
Chambersburg PA
CBHW052212090526
44584CB00019BA/3078